HER JOURNEY
with
A SMILE

The Heartbreak and
The Love After Child Loss

LAURA WHAREPAPA

In Loving Memory

Our darling Ruiha, how we miss having you here with us. There isn't a day that has passed where for a moment we often find ourselves thinking of you.

You gave us so many memories that we will cherish and carry with us throughout our time here on earth and until it is our time to reunite with you again.

Our sweetie pie, please keep sprinkling some magic butterfly kisses over us.

Love you forever xxx

First published by Ultimate World Publishing 2023
Copyright © 2023 Laura Wharepapa

ISBN

Paperback: 978-1-922982-26-1
Ebook: 978-1-922982-27-8

Laura Wharepapa has asserted her rights under the Copyright, Designs and Patents Act 1988 to be identified as the author of this work. The information in this book is based on the author's experiences and opinions. The publisher specifically disclaims responsibility for any adverse consequences which may result from use of the information contained herein. Permission to use information has been sought by the author. Any breaches will be rectified in further editions of the book.

All rights reserved. No part of this publication may be reproduced, stored in or introduced into a retrieval system, or transmitted in any form, or by any means (electronic, mechanical, photocopying, recording or otherwise) without the prior written permission of the author. Any person who does any unauthorised act in relation to this publication may be liable to criminal prosecution and civil claims for damages. Enquiries should be made through the publisher.

Cover design: Ultimate World Publishing
Layout and typesetting: Ultimate World Publishing
Editor: Vanessa McKay

Ultimate World Publishing
Diamond Creek,
Victoria Australia 3089
www.writeabook.com.au

DEDICATION

For my husband Ray and two sons, Toi & Reihana.
I dedicate this book to you
I know the death of Ruiha has impacted you all in so many ways.
It came and went quickly.
It took a piece from your heart.
It forced you to navigate your way through this unknown path called grief.

My hope is that this book will continue to help you in your healing journey. Let it be a gentle reminder that no matter what trials and tribulations we go through in life, there is always a light at the end of the tunnel if we choose to see it.

I love you all so much and I will always be here to help guide you.

Contents

Dedication v

Introduction 1

Chapter 1: In the Beginning 3

Chapter 2: Power of Prayer 9

Chapter 3: Challenges too Young 15

Chapter 4: The Diagnosis 23

Chapter 5: Hospital Life 29

Chapter 6: Unknown Intentions 35

Chapter 7: I'm Dying 39

Chapter 8: Hair Loss 45

Chapter 9: Mother's Day 51

Chapter 10: Death Came 59

Chapter 11: Is this the Circle of Life? 65

Chapter 12: We are Home 71

Chapter 13: A New Day, New Beginning. 77

Chapter 14: A First for Everything 83

About the Author 89

Acknowledgements 93

Glossary 95

Introduction

To you who has had to endure one of the most painful things in life, burying your child and having to carry on with life the best way you know how, I see you. To the brother and sister who have had to bury their sibling, I see you.

I remember looking at my daughter who was only fourteen years old at the time, laying in her hospital bed just staring at the ceiling, no words, just a tear trickling down one side of her face.

Her Journey with a Smile

The sound of our breathing was the only thing echoing in the room and I could feel her pain, it was relentless, it was cutting deep and for the first time as a mother, I couldn't do anything to help take that pain away from her.

I held her hand in mine, I hugged her tighter than ever before and placed a kiss on her trickling tear, but still no word from her, no movement, nothing.

Just minutes before, my daughter had been diagnosed with terminal Rhabdomyosarcoma cancer and we were told our daughter is dying.

Chapter 1

IN THE BEGINNING

I felt overwhelmed when I found out that I was pregnant with my first girl. I was in my early twenties and I was still trying to figure out how to be a mother to my then two year old son.

I was terrified. I had no savings, no stable employment, I didn't even know if my daughter's father was ready to be a dad. But, my biggest fear was the unknown and unexpected possibility of my daughter being left alone in this big world if anything happened to me, the same way my mother had left me at a young age.

My mother passed away when I was fifteen, I am her youngest child and her passing stirred so many unhappy emotions in me at a time when I was not able to decipher the stages of grief. I channelled my grief into just enough mischief for me to get growled at but not into serious trouble. Well at least that's how I remember it? I'm sure there would be someone in my family who has a different story of me lol. It was hard for me to make peace with my mother's death. To be honest, I never did until I experienced the journey with my own daughter. A lot of familiar emotions I remember having when my mother passed resurfaced within me, and cut me deep.

I had a loving dad who did his very best to fill the role of mum for me. My dad had lost so much after my mum's passing, but he and my siblings still managed to put my well-being first. I always felt genuine love from my siblings during this time, they helped me more than they know, so I did often wonder growing up in my teens, what sort of mum I would be to my own children and wondered if I could emanate the same love my sisters had towards me.

In the Beginning

Every time I went for my scans or any appointments to do with my pregnancy, I tried to be happy, I wanted to be happy, well I was sort of happy but there was always that void. Even today, it's hard to describe that void in detail. I guess if you have also been without a mum from a young age, you would know what I mean or what I'm trying to say here. The feeling of abandonment was real for me.

My daughter was born on 11 September 1999. I had woken at 2am that morning with a boost of energy and an urge to start cleaning my house. I was cleaning what had already been cleaned earlier that day. I think the movement actually helped to bring the labour pains on. It all happened so quick and before I knew it, I was cradling my baby girl in my arms. She had big brown eyes and a grin that looked like a smile. She never cried at birth, she just quickly latched at my breast. She was such a content baby from birth. Wow, I said as I looked at her, welcoming my first and only daughter into the world, Shannon Ruiha Patene. Names given to her from her father's side of the family.

Ruiha was just an all-round happy baby, and very easy to care for. I felt very blessed, I had a newborn who let me sleep. That's the important part right? Sleep?

From the age of four her personality started to shine. Ruiha went from being a quiet girl to a full blown chatter box and a snitch to those who did wrong in front of her. Some of my family members would describe her as a mini me. What you saw is what you got from her, facial expressions and all.

When she started school, the name Ruiha replaced Shannon. She attended, Kohanga Reo, a Māori language pre-school in New Zealand that teaches traditional language and customs. The name Ruiha is the name they called her and it stuck with her.

Ruiha loved school, she loved her friends and wasn't a kid who kept to one circle. One teacher described her as a 'social butterfly.' She had friends who came from all walks of life and would often be drawn to those who looked to be struggling with home life. She was the go to friend who her peers trusted with their secrets.

During a teacher interview, her father and I were told that Ruiha had been giving her lunch away to other children and would often go without. We always wondered why she would come home starving after school. I always thought she never liked the sandwiches I made and that she was throwing them in the bin. Now that I think back, I wouldn't have blamed her if she did.

I would make extra lunch for her so she had some for herself, only to be later told by her teacher again, that she would give the extra lunch we sent with her away to other people too. We never growled at our daughter for doing this, instead I encouraged my daughter to help others if she could, but to make sure she kept some food for herself. Ruiha would do this act of kindness for a few years to come, and she did it without expecting anything in return. If there was one quality I had to describe of her, it would be her kindness toward others. She treated people how she wanted to be treated.

She did the same with animals as well, often feeding the strays and bringing them home to care for until they were ready to be let free again. If she had her way, she would have had a farm in our residential street.

Chapter 2

POWER OF PRAYER

Getting ready for school one morning, I was brushing her long thick beautiful brown hair that reached her lower back. It wasn't her favourite thing. It often involved a bit of pulling and untangling, and sometimes ended in tears. But something seemed off this time, she was quiet and when I asked her if she was okay, she shrugged her shoulders to indicate a yes. When I noticed that her face was pale, I asked her again if she was okay, she replied.

'Mum,' and collapsed onto the floor.

I screamed out to my husband who came and scooped her up in his arms and carried her to the car. We rushed her to the hospital. She wouldn't open her eyes, then her eyes rolled back and her breathing became shallow. I kept yelling at my husband to hurry up, something was terribly wrong with her.

We lived a short drive from the hospital so our reaction was to just put her in the car instead of calling an ambulance. On our way, we were stopped by a police officer who was doing a routine check. My husband explained to him we were taking our daughter to the hospital, but the police officer just looked at our daughter and said,

'she doesn't look sick to me.'

At this point my husband is trying to keep calm while pleading with the officer to let us take our daughter to the hospital and if he didn't believe us, then follow us. He didn't follow us, but he did ring the hospital to see if we had told him the truth. A week later the police officer's sergeant would meet with us and apologised for the behaviour of his work colleague. It was an unexpected, unnecessary and stressful experience. We soon moved on from it as our daughter's health was our priority.

Once Ruiha was admitted, her health started to rapidly decline, there were tests after tests and eventually a paediatrician specialist told us Ruiha needed to be transferred to Starship Children's Hospital in Auckland as tests results revealed she had rheumatic fever that had most likely been caused by a streptococcal infection. It was serious. I had never prayed so much in my life. I prayed for my daughter to get well, but I felt like my prayers were not being answered. The ambulance ride up to Auckland took so long. We had to stop a couple of times when the heart monitor attached to Ruiha flat lined. It was a welcomed relief to see Starship Hospital.

Our journey at Starship Hospital had begun. The nurses and doctors working with our daughter and family were amazing. But, when my daughter's condition didn't improve, and she continued to deteriorate fast, her father and I were given the talk from doctors that no parent want.

We were told that Ruiha had two tiny holes in her heart and that, along with rheumatic fever was making her health deteriorate faster. At this point we were told that we may have to be transferred back to our local hospital and wait.

'Wait for what?' I had asked.

'Your daughter may not live,' is the reply we got.

This information was hard to accept and make sense of, but I never doubted for one minute that she wouldn't be able to fight this.

That evening as I packed our belongings in preparation for the early morning transfer back to our hometown, we got word that family and friends there were praying for her full recovery. It's the only thing we had at that point to rely on, we needed a miracle.

It turns out a miracle did happen for Ruiha. The next morning, I had woken from probably the best sleep I had in weeks and there was Ruiha sitting up in her hospital bed drawing pictures. She then got off her bed, which she had been confined to for three weeks at this point and walked up to me and gave me the biggest hug. I was in absolute shock, especially after been told the day before we had to wait to see what happens. She wasn't even able to walk the day before. Her nurse and doctor came into the room and were shocked at how fast things had changed for Ruiha, the doctor said,

'well, you definitely have angels looking after you young lady.'

Ruiha gave a big smile and replied,

'okay lets go home now mum.'

We didn't get to go straight home, we had to be transferred to our home town's hospital where Ruiha would be monitored for at least another three weeks.

Chapter 3

CHALLENGES TOO YOUNG

Teenage years had crept up out of nowhere and before I knew it I had a young lady who was now taller than me, full of life with dreams and I dare say it, boys at the centre of hers and her peers' conversations. I knew I was going to be in for one hell of a ride with this girl and I was ready for it. Well, at least I thought I was.

We had settled into living in Australia. Ruiha enjoyed making new friends at high school, getting involved with sports, particularly netball and had a small circle of friends. Often she would enjoy just hanging out with me at home engaging in deep conversations about life in general. I absolutely loved and cherished these times with her.

Then one day, just out of nowhere we would be faced with yet another health challenge, this one bigger and more aggressive than anything our family had experienced.

'Mum! I have a headache! Where's the Panadol?' she screamed as she was running down the hallway.

'Oh my god, what the hell are you yelling for?' I screamed back at her.

The headaches got unbearable.

'Mum look at me, I'm cross eyed,' she said as she pointed to her eye.

'Oh my god mum look at this eye.'

It didn't take long before we would find ourselves sitting in the doctor's clinic, thinking that Ruiha is just being dramatic, that she just had a minor headache that nothing a few more panadol wouldn't fix.

'Ok I think you're going to be just fine,' the doctor said. 'You may need some glasses, so I suggest you go to Spec Savers to get checked.'

Ruiha and I just burst into laughter as our eyes locked when we heard glasses, her reaction to hearing this was hilarious.

'Oh nah, stuff that!' she exclaimed. 'How am I supposed to wear glasses while playing netball?'

I rolled my eyes at her thinking, yep you are your mother's daughter.

We couldn't get an appointment to get her eyes checked until the following day, so we made our way home. This kid made the drive home so unbearable with her going on and on about how she would have to wear glasses on the netball court, I'm sure I drove through a red light that day just to hurry home and avoid listening to her. She even made a phone call to her father's workplace and told him she needed glasses. We hadn't even made the appointment yet. To say she was being dramatic is a nice way of telling it.

Appointments were made and we were set for the following day. Ruiha had gone to bed early that evening, I thought it may have been because she got tired of complaining. Then unexpectedly, I heard Ruiha run to the bathroom, she was vomiting, so I got up to check to see if she was okay and as I went to open the door to the bathroom, I saw her staring into the mirror. I will never forget the look on her face.

'I'm alright, I think I ate something that's made me sick,' she said.

'Can you lie in bed with me mum?'

I couldn't help but feel like something was wrong, a mother's instinct I'm sure.

Every time Ruiha got sick I think the fear of going through what we did with her when she was younger would instantly kick in. I laid by her until she went to sleep.

The following morning, we went to Spec Savers, Ruiha had got in a huff with me earlier because I told her she wasn't allowed to go to school and that she needed to get her eyes checked. She had got out of bed refreshed, skipping her way into the kitchen dressed in her school uniform as if nothing had happened the night before. I gave her a thumbs up for been eager for school and in return she gave the typical teenager reaction, stomping her feet and slamming her bedroom door. Honestly, it was hilarious to witness her get into tantrums, because she very rarely gave attitude at all.

So here we were sitting at Spec Savers, I paid attention to the optometrist and his facial reactions for some sort of sign or something to indicate whether or not everything was okay.

'Okay mum,' the optometrist said. 'You need to take her straight up to the hospital, please do not delay as its urgent. There is something that looks like a large mass behind the optic nerve that shouldn't be there, please take her to the hospital now.'

'What the fuck?' I replied.

As for Ruiha, she just jumped straight off the bed,

'Cool lets go for a feed now mum! I'm hungry,' she said.

Everything had happened so fast at this point and before we knew it, our family were sitting around our daughter's hospital bed, waiting for a doctor to tell us what was happening with her. As we waited, we were literally watching Ruiha become very sick.

She complained that her headaches were getting worse and that the lights in the emergency area were too bright for her. She was exhausted. The vomiting had started again. I remember feeling really anxious and nervous and just sat in silence, waiting. It felt like we were going down that same path again. The doctors were moving as fast as they could to get results back from an MRI that Ruiha had earlier, they couldn't give her any stronger medications to help ease her headaches and stop the vomiting until they were certain what the cause of her illness was. We were becoming frustrated and impatient. It took hours.

Eventually, Ruiha's dad and I were asked to follow a doctor to a computer screen. Once there, we were shown a picture of the outline of Ruiha's skull. The doctor pointed out the large mass around her optic nerve area, which the optometrists from Spec Savers thought he had seen. The rest of what the doctor said after that was a bit of a blur. I had immediately feared the worst, *oh my god it's a tumour* I thought.

Ruiha had to get a biopsy done to determine what that mass was. Which meant Ruiha needed to be admitted into hospital. I think doctors knew what that mass was but had to do the tests first to make sure they weren't giving us the wrong diagnosis.

Doctors wasted no time now and Ruiha was scheduled to have the biopsy done the following morning. We didn't realise it would take at least two weeks for the results to come back due to the process of testing the biopsy. The waiting made me more anxious and I couldn't imagine what was going through Ruiha's mind at that time too. Unlike the first health problem we went through when she was younger, Ruiha was old enough now to understand and communicate how she was feeling and ask questions about the whole experience.

When a mother intuitively feels deep in her soul something is wrong with her child, believe it to be true.

Chapter 4

THE DIAGNOSIS

The thought of someone poking around in my daughter's head would be the start of many uneasy and emotional experiences ahead. I really had thought all Ruiha needed two weeks ago was some new glasses and maybe an antibiotic and Panadol for the nausea and headaches.

Filling out crosswords, roaming the hospital hallways and eating hospital food for the past two weeks was exhausting to say the least and I was asking every nurse that came into the room,

'How long will we need to wait?'

'Are the results in yet?'

'Where's the doctor?'

'What's happening?'

'Who are you?'

The more questions I asked, the less I saw nurses come into the room, I giggle now when I look back because if I were in their shoes, I probably would have done the same and avoided coming into Ruiha's room too.

I would go on a hunt down the hallways for any nurse or doctor who could give me a straight answer, the response was always the same.

'We need to wait for a doctor.'

Our family were tired, we were now entering our third week and still no biopsy results. At this point our patience was thin, we were starting to get frustrated with each other and bickering at the smallest of things. Then finally…

The Diagnosis

'Hello, I'm a paediatric oncologist. I'm so sorry to have to tell you, your daughter has Rhabdomyosarcoma cancer and there's usually only a small survival rate.'

All I understood was cancer.

'But you can cure her right?' I asked.

'We will do our best to make her feel comfortable, however we have prepared for you all to move to the children's hospital, where there are several tests we need to complete,' he said.

'No not my baby, you have it wrong.' I replied. 'She doesn't have cancer?'

I looked at my daughter, holding her hand as he proceeded to explain to me the next steps and what that will look like for Ruiha and our family in the weeks to come. Ruiha just stared at the ceiling, her eyes filling with tears.

'Mum, can I go home please?' she asked.

These were the only words she said for the rest of the night. I could only imagine what she could have been thinking, I wish I could take it all from her. Sadness filled the room that evening. When told of the news, it was just Ruiha and I in the room at the time and I was still yet to make the phone call that I dreaded to her dad and brothers who were waiting at home for an update.

I quietly got off her bed and walked out into the hallway of the hospital ward. It seemed like I was walking forever down a never ending hallway. I must have looked strangely lost on a hallway I had walked for the past three weeks, because a nurse stopped me and asked if I was okay. I don't think I even replied to her. I just kept walking. I did find a spot where I knew no one would see me or ask questions. I sat with my head in my hands and started weeping. I remember saying my father's name who had been deceased for a few years:

'Dad, why?'

'Dad, I need you to help me please.'

'Why my baby girl?'

I needed my father to tell me everything was going to be all right, just like he did when he was alive. I sat alone for a long time, feeling like I had failed as a mother, it was my job to keep her safe and I failed. All sorts of things were going through my head. I was alone. And it was definitely a time of make or break for me. But as strange as it may seem, I do believe my dad was there with me the whole time comforting me and whispering,

The Diagnosis

'Get up, you got this.'

And that's exactly what I did, I got up from the floor, gathered myself and reached for my phone in my pocket to ring my husband and sons,

'Hun,' I said.

'The doctor said she has cancer.'

The conversation paused and went silent for a moment. I wish I could have reached for my husband to hug him, I felt his pain and anger. This was his baby girl, his only daughter. It didn't take him and our sons long to make their way to the hospital after that phone call. There were no words to explain in depth our family's pain as we embraced each other.

I remember going in for a big hug with my husband and he whispered,

'Everything is going to be all right,' he said. 'Our sweetie (Ruiha) is going to be okay.'

I needed to hear that, we all needed to hear those words and as I walked with my husband and sons back to Ruiha's room, very little was said, we knew we didn't want to upset Ruiha anymore than she needed during this time. But when you saw her laying on her bed, it was hard not to have some sort of reaction. She looked at her brothers with a smile and quietly said to them,

'Hi.'

They looked at her and nodded and said,

'Chur,' in sync, followed by one brother searching in the drawers next to her for lollies whilst the other one sat in his chair scrolling through his phone.

Ruiha then asked them both,

'Didn't you bring anything for us to eat?'

Our kids broke that awkward feeling of seriousness and before we knew it, we were all talking and yelling over the top of each other, just as we did when we were at home.

The hospital staff allowed our family to stay with Ruiha for the night which is not usually something they would agree with. Usually only one person is allowed to stay so we really appreciated them for going out of their way to understand our request to stay with Ruiha. Leaving Ruiha alone after such big news wasn't an option and I'm forever grateful to the staff' for having compassion. It made Ruiha, and the communication between our family and medical staff more comfortable.

Chapter 5

HOSPITAL LIFE

We were well and truly in the midst of everything to do with chaos and it was happening all so fast since the diagnosis three weeks earlier. Ruiha had been transferred from one hospital to the now former Royal Brisbane Children's hospital.

What an eerie hospital this was. Long corridors, sort of scary to walk alone in but as strange as that all seemed, it actually felt quite homely too, especially in the children's oncology ward. It had a full kitchen with a large family room, big enough for several families to enjoy at once. It felt like home. Very different to the new children's hospital Ruiha would later be transferred to. It was an hours drive from our home.

Ruiha had definitely made herself feel at home and enjoyed the attention she got from the beautiful nurses who would spoil her with their kindness. But despite all of the spoils she received, I noticed Ruiha becoming more withdrawn from conversations and becoming less of her talkative self, less of who we knew Ruiha to be. I also started to see the light in her eye's dimmer, I saw her hurting.

Being the girl she was, she never liked to express to others how she was truly feeling. She was good at hiding her emotions even in the most serious of times. I was probably the only person who she ever talked to in depth about everything and it was hard as a mother to do nothing but watch and wait. Life as we came to know it from this point was, living in hospital and living out of bags. I started to forget what our home looked like.

I think we had become so involved in the process of transitioning from home to hospital life, that for a moment we forgot to ask each other how we were doing, and what we were feeling. Things may have been different and helped us deal with what was yet to come, if we had communicated in this way, but that's just an assumption I think, because during this time, despite been told Ruiha had a slim survival rate, I really did believe otherwise. I had believed that the doctors had got it all wrong, a miracle was going to happen and Ruiha would be fine. I had mentally switched off from believing the worst was yet to come.

'Mum I've had enough can I go home now please,' Ruiha asked.

We were in our sixth week of her being in hospital and Ruiha was at her breaking point. Over being in hospital, over everyone who was in her presence daily, over me, basically just over it.

'We can't go home yet Ruiha, you have another operation scheduled,' I replied.

'I don't want another operation mum, I already know what's happening, they don't need to tell me,' she said. 'I just want to go home.'

I knew it would only be a matter of a time before Ruiha would show her frustration, all she wanted was to go home and get a bit of normal back into her daily routine. She was over been looked after by everyone, over the four walls she had been confined to and just had enough at this point.

She wasn't interested in having another operation, she was done.

'Mum tell them I don't want another operation and tell them I'm packing up to go home,' she said.

So, I did exactly what she asked. I told the nurses and her specialists what Ruiha wanted me to say. I did this knowing full well that we wouldn't be allowed to take her home. Ruiha needed to feel like someone was listening to her.

There was a strange legality to the whole situation. There were things we as parents were told we weren't allowed to do: such as when I had asked about alternative medicines because I could clearly see the negative impact that radiation and chemotherapy were having on Ruiha. But I was told, that because Ruiha is a child if I choose to refuse chemotherapy, this could be seen as child neglect and could have severe consequences on us as parents. It made me furious in many ways as I had felt my rights as a parent were being taken away from me. I knew my daughter more than anybody else, how dare they tell me what was best for my daughter. I also understand that there are dangers in going off to find alternative options, especially for a child. But still, I struggle even to this day understanding why I couldn't explore other options. Would alternative medicines have saved her? I will never know, but what I do know, is that radiotherapy and chemotherapy didn't help her.

I found myself dwelling on my frustrations and would bottle them up inside me, until night times while Ruiha was sleeping, I'd find a place to cry. It was hard to tell people how I was feeling as I felt like people wouldn't understand what the magnitude of being told 'your daughter is dying' really felt like. There was nothing good that was going to come from this journey. I thought if there was a hell, I was pretty certain this experience was it for me.

Chapter 6

UNKNOWN INTENTIONS

To tell our story properly, I'm going to have to include the difficulties we experienced when dealing with others, which means having to revisit some ugly truths.

Navigating through choosing battles carefully and to do it without projecting hurt or worry onto Ruiha was our priority, even if it meant doing so while putting on a front. She was already facing enough, so she didn't have to carry adult worries too.

You see, whilst going through all of this, there were people who helped us, from offering cooked meals, to organising events. At the time it all seemed so loving and kind, but not everyone acted with the best of intentions. Most of it we felt was genuine but the reality is, people are people and not everyone is genuinely there to help without expecting something in return. A wolf in sheep's clothing is probably a good term for the people I'm talking about.

There was a lot of money circulating through fundraisers that my husband and I never created, we had no control over who was doing what and what some of the fundraisers were. The ones we did know about, the organisers had asked us first if we would be okay with it, which is a pretty common courteous thing to do right? But then there were those who went off and set up go fund me pages and raffles that were only brought to our attention from people who had contributed to them. Unfortunately, there were also people in corporate positions who pocketed from using our daughter's illness.

The first thing I needed to do was to make contact with the people who were doing these things without our knowledge. When I did this, I always did it with the intention to sort through and do it within reason and love. But I couldn't control how the other person and people would receive and react to it. Ruiha never received any money from these unknown fundraisers. In fact, all monies fundraised without our knowledge were pocketed by these organisers.

There was money, signed memorabilia and gift cards to name a few of the items that these people had pocketed. To say it was hurtful when we found these things out is an understatement. The fact that people would actually scoop so low to insert themselves into my family's situation at the time and literally steal from a dying child, my dying child, is beyond belief. But it happened and had we known we would be facing these things I would have declined every fundraising initiative for Ruiha, for the sake of protecting my family.

Even a year or two after, there are some people who I had eventually had disagreements with, who would say things to me like- after all we did for Ruiha. Wow! Is what I would always say during these times, because here I am thinking everyone helped Ruiha because they genuinely cared for her. Not helped her to expect something in return. How silly was I?

This affected our family and it has made us very weary of receiving even a little help from people, even to this day. Thankfully, our sons haven't changed the way they give to others if they have it. They are still kind boys and will help anyone without expecting anything in return, just as their sister was. I worked hard to keep them from knowing what was happening during this time as well. But they knew and they know everything that went on.

It did take me a while to get over what had happened despite knowing there was someone more important who needed my attention during this time. I had to eventually forgive them, for the sake of my own sanity, but it wasn't easy. Forgiveness is a painful journey and yet such a rewarding and beautiful thing to experience when you know you have truly let that hurt go. I had to let go of the hurt and acknowledge the grief we were in and boy what a mission!

The whole experience has made me not be so quick to trust, even those close. I no longer do circles of friends anymore but instead prefer to stick to dots. Meaning I only prefer to talk to one or two friends and spend time with them. My boundaries have changed a lot. I have deeper and much more satisfying conversations with one on one rather than in a group setting. Once my instincts kick in good or bad, it generally determines my time and how it is spent with people.

In the end, it really did come down to choosing what battles were worth fighting, it also meant I had to navigate my way through a lot of shadow work. It is all a work in progress.

Chapter 7

I'M DYING

'Mum! Let's go to movie world!' Ruiha said.

I'm rolling my eyes thinking what the hell is this girl on?

'I wanna go on the superman roller coaster!' she yelled.

Ruiha had already been told by her specialist that she is unable to do anything strenuous, as it could aggravate the tumour behind her optic nerve.

'What the hell, who cares what they say mum, I wanna go!'

After a lengthy conversation with her specialist, we were told that ultimately it was our choice. So we didn't hesitate to take her to somewhere she wanted to go. Some may say it was stupid of us to do, going against 'professional advice' but let's just leave that and maybe have a face to face conversation at a later time, then I'll be more than happy to sit down and talk about 'professional advice' for my child. It goes back to the saying, you don't know unless you are in this situation.

Ruiha knew she wasn't well, and she would become quite upset when she was told she couldn't do anything because it might make her sicker. She was dying, she couldn't get any worse than that, right? So, I had her back all the way and if there was room for options, I was there helping her find them. Even for what some think is a small thing, like going to a theme park.

I truly believed Ruiha just wanted to feel like she had a bit of normal back in her life, away from the hospital life she had got to know. When I told her we could go to the theme park, she was full of excitement.

I'M DYING

I somehow knew, that Ruiha wouldn't get on the superman ride, that she would change her mind once we got there. She knew how much her body could handle and she knew her limits. She wasn't stupid. All she wanted was a break.

Travelling away from home and hospital with Ruiha, was an exercise for us, it included packing half of the car from the roof to the floor (that's no exaggeration) with her things: a wheelchair; medications; her bags; specific dietary foods and the list goes on. It was like taking a pharmacy on the road with us and nothing ever started off smoothly, it often led into some sort of argument caused by the stress of it all. The laughs and memories during these times however, always outweighed the dramas.

Ruiha had tubes inserted around her heart and thigh areas that needed that extra care whilst away from home or hospital, these were literally her lifelines if they needed to be used to pump medication through in emergency situations. Her immune system was not like ours. We always had to be extra careful, much to her dismay and frustration. She absolutely hated the things but knew how important they were too.

Anyone who has cared for cancer patients would know how cautious and careful one needed to be, hygiene is especially important. But when it's a child or teenager, those rules often fall to the wayside, they don't want life to stop just because they have limitations on the daily and Ruiha was no exception to this. I learnt a lot from watching Ruiha's behaviour and that of other terminally ill children, their outlook on life was very different, they never let their illness stop them from pursuing day to day activities and they did it with happiness. Such a lot of innocence and no worries in the world. They kept moving forward the best way they could.

Heck! some adults think the world has ended because they get a paper cut on their finger. Are you feeling me? LOL.

'Yaaay we are here!' Ruiha yelled.

We could see the superman and the green lantern rollercoasters as we drove into the carpark and the smile on Ruiha's face was a beautiful sight to see, she was overly excited and happy, I was reminded of the little girl she was at heart.

The smells of popcorn and other food tempted us, but food prices at the theme park were a put off, so luckily we had already packed our lunch.

'OMG mum, there it is!' Ruiha said, as she stood in awe watching the superman rollercoaster in action and listening to the screams of the brave people.

'I don't think I'll go on now though.' She said.

I'M DYING

I wasn't surprised and secretly relieved that she decided not to go on, but she was happy to sit a few minutes and watch. I felt really sad for her in that moment as would any other parent in this situation and although she was happy, I also felt her sadness for not being able to do something she had badly wanted to do. I told her one day she will be able to go on it again and she smiled back at me,

'It's ok mum, I got to go on with dad before I got sick and heard dad scream, that's all that matters,' she said laughing.

It was as if she knew that this would be her last visit to the theme park, which turned out to be true.

We spent a couple of hours at the theme park, looking at all the happy little faces running past us. I couldn't say the same about the parents who looked flustered as they chased after their runaway children. I remember thinking, I am so glad I don't have to do that anymore.

When we got hungry we headed out to the car park to eat our lunch. Ruiha had gone into the car to lie down and when I went to check on her she said she wasn't feeling too good. I blamed the heat, and we packed up the car to make our way home.

We hadn't been home long and Ruiha started vomiting profusely, it was almost like watching a repeat of the lead up to her being diagnosed with cancer, but the feeling of watching this play out again felt different. Something was off, but I couldn't pinpoint to what it was.

I helped her into a running cold shower to cool her and It did help the vomiting settle and by this time, she was exhausted.

'Mum I feel different,' she said. 'I'm dying.'

Chapter 8

HAIR LOSS

'Mum, I can't wait for this to be over and done with.'

Ruiha was nearing the end of her radiation and still had a little while before chemotherapy would be finished. Such a gruelling and unapologetic process for any child to go through. Recovery took days after treatments and the time it took Ruiha to bounce back had me worried.

None of this process ever made sense to me, why was poison (as I call it) being pumped into her.

As a parent, I wished I had options in deciding Ruiha's treatments. I also often wished she was an adult who could have made her own decisions and chose whether or not these treatments (chemo and radiation) were right for her. Because if she was an adult during this time, her words and opinions would have mattered. At least she would have been given options. I know she wouldn't have chosen radiation or chemotherapy. She would have sought alternative medicines. With the knowledge we gained while going through this, I would have rather put her through a strict rainbow and detox cleanse than have her suffer poison being pumped into her body.

We couldn't wait for Ruiha to be done with treatments too, she was beyond tired and we had witnessed firsthand, the affects it had on her body, it was harsh and painful to watch our daughter go through it all. As well as the common physical changes from the cancer treatments, the toll on her mental health was a big concern. I was able to recognise signs that would indicate something was off with her and with her not bouncing back as quickly as before, I knew something was happening. I felt that time was ticking.

I remember when she came to me crying, holding a chunk of her hair in her hands. The fear on her face said it all.

Hair Loss

The picture of her during this time is embedded in my mind and often brings me to tears when I think about it.

'Mum please cut my hair, I don't want it.' She cried.

I couldn't imagine how she felt or what was going on in her mind, but after much hesitation I had to cut her hair, I finally agreed to do it and I only did it with the hope it could make her feel a little better. How? I have no idea. Before I knew it I was standing behind her with clumps and single strands of her hair in my hand and I remember thinking, *wow how did we really get to this? Why my child?*

I made the first cut at her neckline, I gasped and stared at her while she stared back at me in the mirror, I hated every moment of cutting her hair and the quieter she got the harder it was to continue.

The sadness in her eyes was unbearable to see, especially when the long length of hair was almost gone, and it became even more surreal when I got the hair shavers out. I couldn't do this part as I was scared I was going to cut her head, so a nurse offered to do it for her. Ruiha at this point was completely silent, I remember taking a photo of her and to this day, I've never looked at that photo again. It's the only photo I have of her since birth that captures sadness, fear, aloness and death in that one moment. It haunted me to see my daughter like that.

It took a while to cut off all her long hair, but once it was gone she sat in front of the mirror taking in the moment. I told her she still looked beautiful, she gave a smile back but was still quiet.

'Mum.' She cried.

I grabbed her and gave her the biggest and longest hug. I wiped her tears, and I reminded her she was beautiful.

'I don't feel like I am mum,' she said.

'I really look like I have cancer now.'

'I'm dying mum.'

The nurse came into the room to sweep the hair off the floor, I asked her to wait until I had picked most of it up myself and put it in a bag. I did this so I could keep her hair and take it home. The thought of her hair being thrown in the rubbish didn't settle with me. I had planned to plait it or possibly make a wig for Ruiha from it as there was enough hair to do it. Ruiha wasn't keen to wear a wig so I decided to buy a nice little keepsake box for it instead.

As time went by, she got comfortable with her new look and found ways to make herself look and feel good. Without her thick long hair there was no need for untangling and brushing knots. It was a relief for me too, no longer having to pick hair up off the bathroom floor and unclogging the shower and sink holes.

Chapter 9

MOTHER'S DAY

'Happy mother's day mum,' Ruiha said, 'I love you.'

These would be the last words I would clearly hear Ruiha say to me, because within a week, everything would quickly spiral downward.

Ruiha and I had arrived at the hospital a couple of days prior to mother's day, because her vomiting was not settling. Her specialist decided it would be best for her to be admitted for observations, she had become quite unwell by this point. She was still alert, but barely talking and withdrawn as if she was falling in and out of constant deep thought. I intuitively knew something about this situation had changed with her but I couldn't decipher it or make sense of what I was witnessing. I would later be told by a specialist that these things that I saw, were in fact, the first signs of Ruiha's body shutting down and that death was knocking at her door and that it was normal behaviour that I was witnessing from a person in their final days. They get a burst of energy with a bit of disorientation before their final moments.

I had imagined we would only be in hospital for less than a week and this time would be no different to any other, all she needed was fluids and an extra dose of medication, before being sent home. This was our normal drill in these situations, so we hadn't given it any thought to what might happen then.

Early that morning (Mother's day), I was woken by the sound of shuffling and a door slamming, it was Ruiha,

'Oops sorry mum,' she said as she was getting back into her hospital bed.

This was followed by a loud thump, it was the trolley that had her tubes and water bag dangling from it. She had rammed and pushed it into her bedside drawer out of frustration. Because it got in her way of getting into bed.

'Grrr can't wait for them to take these damn things off me,' she growled.

She had just returned to her room after roaming the ward to chat with nurses doing their midnight rounds with other patients. I must have been in a deep sleep because I hadn't heard her leave the room during this time. I was later told she had made herself comfortable in the nurse's station, played with the nurses landline phones, scribbling on whatever piece of paper that was infront of her and had taken her packet of chocolate freddos to share with the nurses. She had played cards with the nurses and had conversations with them about how she couldn't wait to return to our hometown in New Zealand and go swimming.

Ruiha had told the nurses a fairy-tale like story about having a happy childhood swimming and talked a lot about her grandfather she was raised with.

'He's my angel.' she had told them.

The nurses who cared for Ruiha became our good friends, they always went over and above their job description to ensure the children and their families on the ward were well taken care of. They are the angels that walk this earth.

They helped Ruiha make me a mother's day card, that read:

> *Happy mother's day mum, thank you for everything you have done for me*
>
> *I love you forever*
>
> *p.s- If you don't want that chocolate I'll eat okay lol*
>
> *Love Ruiha xxxx*

I giggled and gave her a kiss on her cheek as she handed me the card, while realising it was 3am.

'Mum are you tired?' She asked.

'Yes, it's only 3am,' I replied.

'I'm tired too mum, very tired. I'm not scared anymore mum.'

'I would be tired too Ruiha roaming the ward and chatting with the nurses at this time.' I replied. I then looked at her with a small slant and asked her what she meant by saying I'm not scared anymore.

'It's ok mum I'm going to be alright, go back to sleep.' she laughed.

MOTHER'S DAY

I wasn't impressed, this kid wakes me up at 3am, starts a conversation and casually tells me to go back to sleep as if it was easy to do. I was unable to go back to sleep, instead I got into bed with Ruiha and we laid in her bed chatting until her eyes got heavy.

'I love you and dad mum.' As she yawned closing her eyes.

'We love you too Ruiha.' I said.

Hours had passed since Ruiha went to sleep, I had been awake since 3am, but now that it was well after midday, I started to get a bit worried she hadn't woken. I tried to wake her a handful of times and was relieved when she pushed my hand away and growled.

I told her it was time to go for a bath, she groaned and without expecting it, she suddenly, just sat upright in bed, never said a word and looked dazed at the wall in front of her. It took a while for me to help her get up and out of bed, It felt like I was lifting dead weight and I started to get worried when she became lethargic and unstable on her feet.

She could still understand what I was saying, but her body couldn't react and never had the energy to communicate. Things were starting to get weird.

Getting Ruiha from her bed to having a bath took over an hour, I couldn't fully understand what was happening to her or why the sudden change in her. Maybe it was because I didn't want to believe it? I'm not sure. But I do know that from what I saw and what I was starting to feel, was different this time. I remember, when she was in the bathtub, I had only turned my back on her for a few seconds and she started slipping under the water, like a little baby not knowing how to keep their head up. I went into full panic mode and immediately let the water out of the bathtub and lifted her out on my own. I could have pushed the big red emergency button on the wall that would have had the nurses running in to help, but in that moment I did what I needed to, and I wanted to keep Ruiha's dignity. I was never comfortable exposing Ruiha even during these times.

It was like her life energy had completely been zapped out of her and all I had in front of me, was just Ruiha's physical body. She couldn't even speak words at this point and had become completely mute.

Once I got Ruiha back into her room and in bed, I got to have a little breather and it was a welcomed relief. I felt exhausted from having been awake since the early hours. But concern and worry started to consume me as I looked at Ruiha laying in her bed, her eyes half open, she can see but there is no communication at all. I had asked a nurse what was happening with her, why is she no longer talking,

MOTHER'S DAY

'I will get a doctor to come and talk with you,' was the reply.

The nurse had not long left the room and as I leaned in to kiss Ruiha's forehead she suddenly started convulsing, her eyes were rolling and her whole body shaking. I got a hell of a fright and hit the red emergency button above her bed and within seconds the room was filled with a doctor from every specialised area within the hospital and all the nurses from the ward. They had all surrounded Ruiha's bed as I was gently grabbed by the arm and taken to the farthest corner of the room. I could no longer see Ruiha without standing on tip toes to see over doctor's and nurse's shoulders. As they started talking doctor language with big words, the energy in the room changed, some doctors looked back at me with sadness and as they each made their way out of the room, each and every one of them placed their hand on my shoulder saying,

'you have a very brave and beautiful girl.'

I will never forget this moment and the way they made me feel. There beside Ruiha's bed was only one doctor, one of the children's oncologist. She had asked if I could ring my husband who had been at work and ask him to make his way up to the hospital within the next few hours as she needed to discuss with us palliative care for Ruiha.

'Huh? Palliative care?'

Chapter 10

DEATH CAME

'If it is your will, open the floodgates of heaven for her lord.'

As the minister spoke those words, Ruiha took her last breath and closed her eyes 12 May 2015. The most excruciating, painful time in my life happened in that moment, it is also the most beautiful memory that I have of my daughter's final time here with us too. Just like that, she was gone, she no longer had to endure pain or months of taking medications, she was free from it all and I am blessed I got to witness and be a part of something spiritual.

I laid next to my daughter soon after and I started to feel the warmth from her body slowly disappear. This would be the turning moment for me when I realised, she wasn't going to wake up and say, '*hi mum,*' ever again.

I felt like my heart had been ripped to pieces and it was getting harder to breathe. It immediately took me back to when my mum had passed and just thinking about it, was making me feel irritated. I also realised I was starting to come out of the initial shock, and I needed to face what had just happened, something I don't think any parent could do in these circumstances. While I could hear people talking around me, hugging and comforting me, I vaguely remember all of those things happening in detail, during the first few hours of Ruiha's passing. I only remember feeling numb, alone, confused and then angry.

By early morning, her body was freezing cold and stiff, rigor mortis had set in. I got her favourite fluffy blanket and I put it over her, just as I would when I would tuck her in bed to keep her warm throughout the night. The colour in her face was also different, so I would stroke the side of her face with the hope she would feel my warmth and she would know, I hadn't left her side. I held her cold hand

Death Came

in mine with the hope I may feel the slightest movement from her, even though I knew that would be impossible, but I had hope. Although I knew my daughter had passed, I still treated her the same as if she were alive. I talked to her, I sang softly in her ear, and I held her tight with the promise I was never going to let her go. I wanted to make sure I was with her every minute until it was time for her to be taken to the funeral home for preparation to travel back to New Zealand. I couldn't bring myself to leave her side, not even when the funeral director said they were ready to take her from the hospital. My family and those around us, were so patient with me and they waited until I was ready to leave the hospital and be comfortable leaving Ruiha in the care of strangers. I just needed to know my daughter was going to be okay.

My time alone with her was also important for me and I probably became a bit selfish in not wanting to share her with anyone or leave anyone alone with her. I also knew that once we stepped foot back onto our marae (Maori land/area with ancestral meeting house) in New Zealand, she would no longer just be mine and my families but instead she would have returned home to our iwi, our tribe, our people. Her funeral would be celebrated with Maori traditions upheld and customed to my tribe over three days before her burial.

Tangihanga in my culture is often a beautiful experience to be a part of and death isn't treated as taboo for those of us who have been fortunate enough to be raised on our marae as kids. Its where the elders of my tribe speak in our native tongue, such beautiful orators can be heard and seen during this time. The women also have very significant roles, in my tribe, they are the first point of call and the first person you will see before you are welcomed onto the marae. If you are a visitor, you can't actually enter onto the marae until she is ready to call you on. It's an eerie call, a beautiful call called karanga, to welcome people, that is then exchanged with a karanga from another woman coming onto the marae with visitors. It's a call that will give you goosebumps. We welcome the multitude who come to pay their condolences to the deceased and their families. It's a ceremony of mourning and laughter, a lot of talk and singing that ends with a large hakari (feast) to feed the visitors and also our families who have worked tirelessly in the kitchen over the three days.

Despite knowing I would be taking Ruiha home to my iwi where they would be waiting for us with open arms and because it was the right thing for me to do. I just couldn't bring myself to accepting the fact she was gone, so all of that never meant anything to me at that time. I wasn't in the right headspace to be making or planning her journey home. I just wanted more time with my daughter, and I wanted to do it alone.

Ruiha had been taken to the funeral home, we went to our home to prepare our journey back to New Zealand, but it was going to take another two days before we could get flights. This was partly due to the paperwork that is required for the funeral home to make the arrangements. This gave my husband and I time to sort through our finances and sit with our two sons and immediate family and discuss how we were going to make this work. One of the downsides to living abroad is when we have to deal with a death in the family. Unlike back in New Zealand, we don't have immediate access to our families who are the go to people in these situations, nor do some of us have the finances to get our loved one's home.

When we moved to Australia, one of the best pieces of advice given to my husband and I was to get funeral insurance if we intended for our families to get us back to New Zealand should we pass away. Doing so would take the financial pressure off our families. So, we did, and never did we think we would be using it within three years after moving to Australia for our own child. Having this plan took such a big financial burden off us and our family's shoulders.

Money, is the last thing any family going through the death of a loved one wants to deal with. The process of receiving the money was smooth, it was given to us by a cheque that we had to deposit into our bank. Lucky for us the funeral insurance company banked with the same bank as us, however that still didn't mean the money would be cleared within forty-eight hours. Cheques usually take seven days to clear. Panic started to set in as we didn't want Ruiha to be in a funeral home, or alone, longer than she needed to be. I also worried that by the time we took her back to New Zealand, we wouldn't be able to have a three day 'tangi' for her, as her body would start to deteriorate.

Thankfully we had the most amazing customer service representatives from our bank who helped clear the cheque within twenty four hours after they had made phone calls to their head office. We were so grateful and happy that side of the financials had been sorted. The sense of relief knowing we could leave Australia with Ruiha and that we had no funeral expenses hanging over our heads was a blessing.

Chapter 11

Is this the Circle of Life?

Ruiha would not return from the funeral home until the following day and this would be the first time since the beginning of her journey, she wasn't around us. I struggled with this, I felt like I had abandoned her and that she would be all alone. I wanted so bad to stay at the funeral home with her, but I also knew that there was so much work to be done in preparing for her final journey back to New Zealand. I also had two sons and a husband who needed me just as much as I needed them.

First task was to find clothes for Ruiha to be dressed in, I hated every part of that. I remember walking around the shops and stopping often to gasp at the pressure of feeling overwhelmed, completely lost and I would ask my husband,

'why are we even doing this?'

It felt wrong for so many reasons.

'I should be shopping with my daughter, not shopping for clothes for her to be buried in.'

I thought, how sad it was to be shopping for clothes to be buried in. Is this what they called the circle of life? How? When it's a child who hasn't even lived a life?. I felt as though we had been handed the wrong deal. The people around me noticed the frustration, anger and resentment that filled me.

It seemed like hours of roaming around looking for that impossible to find perfect outfit for her. In the end we found Ruiha a beautiful long white nightie and a pink fluffy soft robe, one that I imagined would keep her warm and cosy.

Is this the Circle of Life?

'That's it,' I said. 'That's perfect for my sleeping princess.'

Going through her belongings later that evening was another task that needed to be done and was hard to do in such little time. I wanted to pack her bag with things that she would have liked, a bag or two that would be buried with her. Sorting through it all was a big mission, she had accumulated so many things, as teenage girls do. Letting go of her things was almost impossible to do, because all of a sudden, I felt I wanted to keep everything of hers and not part with any of it, It was all I had left of her, so even her pencil case with her pens and other little nik naks became precious to me.

That night felt like an eternity, I laid on her bed beside my husband in darkness, taking in whiffs of smell from her pillow, wishing so much this was all a bad dream. I missed her so much.

We were both emotionally exhausted with what was happening, such an emotional and overwhelming pain that could never be measured and compared to any other loss of a loved one. We both held each other, shared our tears and struggled to believe, that our only daughter has died. How did we get here?

One day we are getting ready to go to a rugby game, the next day my daughter is fighting for her life, then dies. How does one comprehend?

We waited anxiously the next day for that call from the funeral home, to say Ruiha is ready to be picked up. I got to spend my last final moments with her alone in a private room, as I changed her. This time for me I will hold dear to my heart. There she laid, she looked beautiful and at peace. The funeral director had done a brilliant job taking care of her and for that I will always be grateful. She didn't look different and there were no shocks for us when we got to see her, so that made our family a little bit happy. I knew when I looked at her, she was ok.

We waited a few more minutes after I changed her, for the funeral director to place her in her coffin. Seeing our daughter in a coffin, pretty much made everything real for us. This was now a reality for us, real as in, we would no longer be able to hug and hold her physically close to us ever again, that cut us deep. Now we could only lean over her coffin and place kisses upon her cheek or reach in and try to grab her hands. But we had her back with us, that's all that mattered.

We were finally taking her home from the funeral home, the drive had seemed longer than usual and when we drove up our street, there were lines of cars and people all over our home and on the sidewalks, such a beautiful sight to see the many people who had come to pay their respects to our family, especially for Ruiha. We never realised the impact her journey had on people, it was surreal. Such a beautiful welcome home for our daughter and a beautiful memory for us to cherish. We were welcomed with traditional protocols pertaining to our culture, a gentle and proud moment of who we are, and this prepared us in some way for the journey home to New Zealand.

Over the next day we had people come to say their last farewells to Ruiha before her return back to the funeral home for her final preparation for our flight to New Zealand. We wanted her friends to spend time with her and it was so beautiful to witness the love they had for our daughter. I got to meet many of her friends I hadn't met before, also a couple of teachers who came to pay their respects. We got to hear the many stories about Ruiha and how she was at school, we weren't surprised at all to hear of the kindness that she gave toward others, she hadn't changed that side of her from when she was a young girl. The ongoing outpour of love was absolutely beautiful and left an impression on our hearts.

Chapter 12

WE ARE HOME

I took a big gasp and looked back at Ruiha's coffin with tears of relief.

'We are home Ruiha.' I whispered to her.

Back with our iwi, our people, such a special and sad occasion all in one. She had a beautiful send off and the three day formalities had gone by so fast, it was over, we had buried our girl in our family urupa (cemetery). There she was in her final resting place. *Now what?*

Everyone has gone home and resumed their daily lives-

What do we do?
How do we carry on with ours?
Will it ever be the same again?
Do I have to go back to Australia?

I don't want to leave Ruiha behind, I can't...

Before we knew it three weeks had passed since the burial, and it was nearly time for us to return to Australia, my husband and I tried our best to avoid discussing it. But it had to happen. We kept getting reassured by family members that Ruiha is okay, she would want us to go home and start a new journey, only difference is, she wouldn't be with us in the physical sense, but she will always be with us in spirit and in our hearts. These were not really the words we wanted to hear from people who had never buried a child themselves, but I knew those people meant well and believed it wasn't their intentions to hurt us when saying these things. But in the early stages, these are the wrong things to say to a grieving parent. It is probably just going through one ear out the other and not really registering in our heads, but we always remember how people make us feel during these times.

We are Home

A family member had asked to speak with us, we knew straight away what it was going to be about, so we met and reluctantly discussed when we would go back to Australia and although I thought at that time it would be a good idea for us to move back to New Zealand so we could be closer to Ruiha, our jobs were in Australia, we had made a home there and our youngest son was at school. So whatever decision was to be made, either way, we knew we would have to leave Ruiha and return to Australia.

I had even asked my husband to go ahead and leave me back in New Zealand, that way at least one of us would be with Ruiha. I wasn't even thinking about my two sons, nor did I think about my husband when I had asked him to consider that. I was in my own la la land and all I wanted was to be left alone. I couldn't bring myself to leave and still to this day, leaving her behind is one of the most heartbreaking decisions we have had to make.

The day arrived, my husband and two sons were quiet, I was pacing the house hoping the time would just damn well stop. I even hoped we would get notification our flights had been cancelled.

'I don't want to leave Ruiha behind. Please.' I cried.

The drive to the urupa (cemetery) was long, even though it usually takes five minutes from our family homestead and as I walked toward Ruiha's grave, I couldn't hold back my tears. Everything still felt raw for us, in my mind, Ruiha would still be fresh to touch and hug and now the thought of her laying six feet below ground terrified me. I wondered if she was warm, I thought about whether or not she would be screaming for help to let her out. The first few weeks without her I was riddled with worry about her been alone. We spent as much time as we could at her graveside, before making our way to Auckland to catch our flights back to Australia.

The moment I turned my back from her grave and started to walk toward the gate, I instantly felt guilty for leaving her. I had promised her I wouldn't leave her, but now I was. As the car got further away from the urupa, I remember letting out a big yell for Ruiha,

'No please take me back!' I pleaded with my husband.

'I can't do it. I can't leave her.' I kept saying.

The further we drove away from her, the louder my cries got. My husband and sons were just as upset as I was. None of us could make sense of what was happening. It happened all too fast for us, we just needed more time.

We never spoke a word until we were almost at the international airport which was a three hour drive away from Ruiha.

We are Home

'We will be landing in Brisbane in approximately ten minutes and...' is what the pilot said.

That's all I remember hearing since walking through customs back in Auckland. Everything had been a blur since we had left Ruiha's grave. I must have fallen asleep from exhaustion on the flight back to Brisbane or completely shut off. In a world of my own, is probably a good way to put it. We now had to go home without Ruiha, to what I imagined was a cold, lonely, eerie and dark house.

We didn't know what to expect.

When we got home, we knew we had already had our home blessed, a normal ritual for families in Māori culture. It is also done with family after the deceased has been buried. The immediate family will generally return to the place where the deceased passed and the home they lived in. Every family have their own way of doing this.

The moment we opened the door, the warmth that welcomed us was beautiful, there was absolute calmness in the air. We felt then and there, Ruiha was there with us in spirit too. It was nothing like how I had imagined it to be just hours before. Our sons felt comfortable to be back home and that evening we all had what felt like the best sleep in months.

Chapter 13

A New Day, New Beginning

A new day begins, a couple of months have passed and we were trying to get back to putting a bit of 'normal' in our home. Whatever the hell normal looked like then.

My husband and I invested our time with work and ensuring our sons were doing okay, the best way we could, we did this instead of talking about everything that had happened and this was probably the first mistake we made. Not talking with each other about or unpacking what had happened created distance between us and we found ourselves dealing with grief in our own way and on our own. We were in our own bubbles, watching everyone and everything else around us move by fast. It always felt unfair that I could see people happy and yet here I was suffering in silence wanting to scream out loud. Most of the times I really did feel I was asking for help, but no one asked me if I needed it. But the reality was no one knew how to ask, in fear that they may say something wrong. I felt stuck with no one to talk to who would understand, so I went to my general practitioner to ask for help and was referred to a grief counsellor.

I'm not even sure at that point if I was ready to talk to a counsellor, but I went and that session lasted less than forty minutes. It cost money to just sit and talk and it didn't help when I could see the counsellor looking at her watch every few minutes as if to say,

'we need to finish this session before my next client arrives.'

This was the first put off for me.

My grief was compared to the counsellor's experience, with how she lost a friend, I sat there opposite her and said, 'but have you buried your child?.'

'No but I completely understand your situation,' she replied.

In that moment I frowned at her and said some things I probably shouldn't have, but to compare a friend's death to the death of my child was probably the stupidest thing a professional could do.

'I just want to make it very clear, there is no comparison between the loss of your friend and how it made you feel, to the loss of my daughter and how I'm feeling.'

Needless to say, that was the first and last time I went to a grief counsellor.

I walked away angry and more frustrated. I had wanted so bad to find a solution to move forward and to get rid of this dark side of grief that was starting to consume me.

I kept thinking about how I was going to fix my family, probably another mistake as I look back. I tried to fix everything and everyone else around me, instead of looking at myself and this went on for a few years. At the time I thought it was the only way I was going to overcome my grief. It was very emotionally exhausting.

My daily tasks included dropping my youngest son off to school, waving goodbye to my husband who went to work, closing my house up so it would be dark and fighting the urge to not resort to alcohol or getting my hands on dope. I wanted anything to get rid of the pain, while a little voice in my head kept saying, *No Laura, don't do it.*

Honestly, I thought I was mentally starting to go down a dark rabbit hole. I felt I was going crazy. I would cry for hours a day and wipe my tears when it was time to pick my son up from school. I had started to analyse my daughter's whole journey and found ways to blame myself and others as to why my daughter had died:

What if I did this?

What if I didn't do this?

I should have fought harder for her.

It's my fault she is dead.

I tried my best to be present with my family, but the overwhelming guilt and belief that I wasn't allowed to be happy again played with my mental health and some days were good, others not so much. Is this what child loss really felt like?

A New Day, New Beginning

My sons could see me becoming a person who they'd never seen before, and they were no longer sure how to communicate with me and were probably worried about how I would react. Although I hadn't become violent or verbally abusive, my withdrawal toward my family was an eye opener for them and a learning experience for me navigating my way through this thing called grief. I wasn't there for them the way I should have been or the way they wanted me to be and this has had a detrimental affect on my sons and it has been through the grace of God that we could get through this as a family. We pretty much had no choice in the end but to talk to each other about what happened to their sister.

As I continued to find ways to get through day by day without being distant, there was one day I had received a knock at the door. I couldn't hide in the room because the person at the door saw me walking down the hallway at that exact time, it was my friend. One of those friends who I had previously spent very little time with. I was a bit surprised, and I took a deep breath and said to myself, *I'll tell her I'm going out*, so I wouldn't have to sit and talk to her. I wasn't ready to share, and I also didn't want to revisit the memory of Ruiha passing away. She wouldn't leave even after I gave her the first hint.

As our conversation progressed, I started to let my guard down for the first time since Ruiha's passing. Not once did she ask about what had happened, all her questions were directed at me and she genuinely wanted to know how I was doing, she sat with me and listened. I never felt for one moment that her intentions for visiting me were bad. She never tried to insert her own opinions, feelings or compare my situation or cut me off while I was talking and say,

'I understand.'

She just let me talk. I really do feel it was as if god had sent an angel that day, because I will always remember that day as been the most content I had felt in a long time. Something changed in me while being in her presence and for the first time in a long time I started to feel the layers of bricks I had built around my heart, slowly crumble away. I started to believe that I could get through this.

I knew it was going to be a hard journey at that point to understand and navigate my way through the different stages of grief. All I knew, is that I never wanted to stay grieving, and I had to learn how to be gentle in allowing the process to happen naturally without it been forced. Knowing who I could talk to was just as important.

Chapter 14

A First for Everything

The first birthday, first Christmas, first new year, all the first of everything without Ruiha had passed. These times were hard to get through and every significant date that has gone by since that has Ruiha attached to it, is a reminder of what use to be. I have often questioned the saying 'time heals' and all I can say in regard to that, is that in my experience, the years that go by, still brings some level of sadness for me. I say this because every birthday that rolls around, Ruiha would have been 'this age'. She would have had a boyfriend, she would have become the nurse she always wanted to be. I don't ever think this sadness will ever change, but does time heal? I truly believe it does.

Has it changed me? It absolutely has, I have come to realise the true meaning of 'life is too short' and there isn't a day that goes by that I am not constantly reminding myself of that.

Sometimes I have felt like I am reliving it all over again while other times I am celebrating what I have in the now. It's always different.

It's been a journey of healing for the most part and it hasn't been easy. Nor did anyone say it would be. There's nothing glamourous about it, life still goes on and with that comes many of life's woes, many trials and having to navigate my way through. Time didn't stop just because my daughter had passed away, it kept ticking and people kept moving about their own way.

I went through a lot of stripping and breaking down of unforgiveness toward myself and others, constantly chipping away at the things that were no longer contributing to my life in a positive way. This even included separating myself from family members. I knew that separation would only be for a season and I knew that some seasons would take a little bit longer for me to reconnect, with the people I love and I was okay with that.

Talking to people about the different grieving stages has helped and one thing I have had in common with other mum's who have experienced child loss, is that the grieving stages are the same but not in the same order and despite our children passing away under different circumstances, we still go through the same stages and emotions. Denial, anger, bargaining, depression and acceptance are the most common stages and isn't it strange that out of these powerful words that have some sort of negative connotation attached to them, only one stands out to me as been positive and that's acceptance.

Acceptance is where I can confidently say I am in my journey. It has taken time to get to this point and a lot of taking a good look at my life to identify any negative triggers that could keep me stuck in grief. I got to the point where I needed to find myself again and I did that by reconnecting to my roots and my whakapapa (genealogy). It meant having to take that journey back to New Zealand to visit my daughter's and parents grave and sit next to them and just talk by myself. Talk about anything. Lucky for me a few steps away from the cemetery is our wharenui (ancestral meeting house), where I was also able to sit and breathe and be present with my surroundings. The carvings that depict my ancestors and ancient stories, the photos of my elders who have passed on the back wall of the wharenui I felt it all, just by sitting and being in the present moment. I felt in my heart this is exactly what I needed so that I could remember who I was and find my purpose again. I am very blessed to be a part of a culture that I can reconnect to my tupuna (ancestors) through whakapapa that gives me strength to keep moving forward. Going home to New Zealand and having taken those first steps to a healing process was a spiritual shift for me and it worked so well with my mental health. I came back to Australia after that trip, with a new outlook on life and I knew it would be a hard road ahead, with a lot of shadow work on myself, navigating my way through the ugly and painful parts about me.

I know that I wasn't given this journey because I couldn't handle it. I was given it because I could. I am now at a place where I have accepted what happened with Ruiha and by doing so, it has lifted years of grief off me, including the grief I still held for my mother. I have mended relationships with people who I pushed away and have become very cautious and alert on who I allow to speak over my life. I have set boundaries for myself, something I never had done before.

This journey is helping me raise awareness, talk about child loss, challenges, and coming through the grieving stages that I had as a Māori woman.

The pain is no longer attached, but sometimes I remember beautiful moments I shared with Ruiha that takes me back to a certain feeling, and sometimes I still shed tears for her.

Grief has shaken the hell out of me, it has made me sick at times and the pain almost killed my soul. It's taken me on a journey through the darkest places I had never been before, a journey of forgiving, a journey of learning, a journey of promises, a journey of reconnection and identity. And it's all been, 'Her journey with a smile.'

Ecclesiastes 3-8 KJV

To everything there is a season, and a time to every purpose under the heaven:

² A time to be born, and a time to die; a time to plant, and a time to pluck up that which is planted;

³ A time to kill, and a time to heal; a time to break down, and a time to build up;

⁴ A time to weep, and a time to laugh; a time to mourn, and a time to dance;

⁵ A time to cast away stones, and a time to gather stones together; a time to embrace, and a time to refrain from embracing;

Her Journey with a Smile

⁶ *A time to get, and a time to lose; a time to keep, and a time to cast away;*

⁷ *A time to rend, and a time to sew; a time to keep silence, and a time to speak;*

⁸ *A time to love, and a time to hate; a time of war, and a time of peace*

END

ABOUT THE AUTHOR

Born and raised in Aotearoa New Zealand, Laura Wharepapa has had the blessing of being immersed in her Māori culture, learning the different customs and protocols that are centred around her tribal affiliations.

Laura hails from Ngati Pikiao, Ngati Whakaue, Whakatohea. Ngati Maniapoto and Te Atiawa which are tribal areas within the north island of Aotearoa.

Creative, biography, education and history profile writing has always been a passion of Laura's and it all started as a young girl when she was awarded first prize for writing a story about 'The Patupaiarehe by my window' for a school competition. However, her inspiration to continue to write came from falling in love with a book called Pounamu Pounamu written by well-known Māori Author Witi Ihimaera. Laura would be inspired by many other Maori authors, educators, historians and orators from different paths. Her true love for storytelling came from her elders who told stories verbally on their marae, who spoke with grace and confidence, speaking the language that was passed down from generations to generations. Laura's father who was her biggest supporter also helped Laura write a book for his own keeping "Uenuku Mai Rarotonga" a history into the ancestral carvings and meeting house that still stands today.

Laura went on to study journalism and communications where she obtained advanced qualifications, she then went on to write news stories for local newspaper outlets and was a part of a journalism team producing a Māori media magazine for her local tribe. Although she had the opportunity to further her skill in television and radio, Laura wanted to pursue other areas instead where she could still apply her writing skills. She went on to a local environment conservation role where she was appointed communications officer.

ABOUT THE AUTHOR

Fast forward many years, Laura has since moved to Australia pursuing other goals and initiatives, but her writing has still continued away from news media and has steered her towards writing books. The flame that once burned as a little girl and the book that inspired her to continue to write and become an author has been reignited.

Her first book is just the beginning of what's to come. Her Journey with a Smile, is a different perspective about what we think grief should look like. Its real and raw and its honest.

Introducing Laura Wharepapa.

Acknowledgements

There are many people who helped in so many ways during our journey. I would like to acknowledge, give thanks and love to our families and friends, our daughter's amazing care team. The beautiful nurses who are without a doubt, angels who walk this earth.

To our koeke, my elders I love and appreciate you all. Beautiful orators, singers with a wealth of knowledge who continue to maintain our customs, so that we may never lose sight of who we are and where we belong. The hard work you all do for our Iwi, our hapu (tribes) and you all never expect anything in return.

Our families who worked tirelessly over the duration of our daughter's tangihanga (funeral), we are forever grateful, and the work done will never be unnoticed from me and my family, especially to each and every person who worked hard in that wharekai.

We thank each person who gave koha (donations) whether it was money, time, or the food to feed the multitude.

And last but not least, my husband and two sons for everything we have been through, what a blessing it is to still have each other.

Nga mihi nui kia koutou katoa
Laura

Glossary

Kohanga Reo	Māori language Pre School
Marae	Sacred Māori land/area with ancestral meeting houses
Iwi	Tribe
Tangihanga	Funeral
Karanga	Calling
Hakari	Feast
Tangi	Cry
Urupa	Cemetery
Whakapapa	Family genealogy
Wharenui	Ancestral meeting house
Tupuna	Ancestors, elders who have passed, chiefs.
Koeke	Elders
Wharekai	Dining room

www.ingramcontent.com/pod-product-compliance
Lightning Source LLC
Chambersburg PA
CBHW030042100526
44590CB00011B/306